Big C, little ta-ta

Janet Sheppard Kelleher

DEDICATION

Merrie Christmus – the caregiver God gave me who stayed by my side every minute, despite how difficult or disgusting. I'm not sure I would have made it without my selfless friend.

Rosemary Lambert Falls – As fine a doctor as ever breathed shot my tumors with both barrels—and kept me kicking to tell the story! I owe her my life.

Barbara Price – my English Literature teacher not only said I had a book in me, but also convinced me that I could and should write it. I owe her a debt I cannot pay.

Cappy Hall Rearick – the amazing and talented mentor taught me that my forte is nonfiction and the story of my life should be told one snapshot at a time.

ACKNOWLEDGMENTS

I'd like to express my sincerest appreciation for the encouragement graciously given me by these dear souls: Amy, Anna, Barbara, Betty, Brenda, Buzz, Cheryl, Chris, CW, Deborah, Edna, Eleanor, Faye, Flo, George, Gwen, Hal, Holly, Inez, Janet, Janey, Janice, Julie, Julia, Katherine, Kelly, Kenzie, Leslie, Linda, Lynn, Maggie, Margie, Mary, Mamie, Martha, Melissa, Meredith, Mike, Nancy, Pam, Patty, Paula, Pinkoner, Ruth, Sandra, Sarah, Shari, Sheila, Terri, Vernecia, Vicki.

The support and recognition of the importance of this memoir by my loving husband Ed (Irish) proved invaluable. The creativity, love, and enthusiasm of my children—David,

Sarah, and Julia—kept me happy, entertained, and youthful.

To Debra Brown, Meredith Brown, Rosemary Gray, John Alexander, and Doy Cave—your contribution, professionalism, tenacity, and expertise made this dream come true.

The advice from my critique group kept me searching for the right words.

The Cayce-West Columbia Library staff kept me focused by granting me the use of their distraction-free Study Room #4.

My church family kept me inspired.

The following poem is for all of you who encouraged me—named and unnamed—your influences made all the difference in the world.

TOUCHING SHOULDERS

There's a comforting thought at the
close of the day,
When I'm weary and lonely and
sad,
That sort of grips hold of my crusty
old heart
And bids it be merry and glad.
It gets in my soul and it drives out
the blues,
And finally thrills through and
through.
It is just a sweet memory that
chants a refrain
"I'm glad I touched shoulders with
you!"
Did you know you were brave, did
you know you were strong?
Did you know there was one
leaning hard?
Did you know that I waited and
listened and prayed,

And was cheered by your simplest
word!
Did you know that I longed for that
smile on your face,
for the sound of your voice ringing
true?
Did you know I grew stronger and
better because
I had merely touched shoulders
with you?
I am glad that I live, that I battle
and strive
For the place that I know I must fill;
I am thankful for sorrows, I'll meet
with a grin
What fortune may send, good or ill.
I may not have wealth, I may not
be great,
But I know I shall always be true,
For I have in my life that courage
you gave
When once I rubbed shoulders with
you.
—Unknown

Janet Sheppard Kelleher

CONTENTS

Acknowledgments   ii

Introduction   1

An Ancient Prayer   3

Get a Transfer   5

Miss America or Misadventure   7

The Braid of Affliction   15

Baseballs, Boobs, Biopsies and   25
Belly Laughs

Two Sizes Too Small   33

I Left My Heart in San Francisco   39

Home-Brewed Tattoos   45

The Tattered Ta-Ta   53

Things to Remember   59

It Couldn't Be Done   67

I Continue to Buy Green Bananas   71

INTRODUCTION

"Cancer sucks. There's nothing about cancer that doesn't suck." WRONG! That quote is from the web site, "How to Kill Your Imaginary Friends."

I thought about that statement for a long time. As a 2000 cancer victor, I learned that humor benefits us in our treatment. It may not cure the disease, but it goes a long way toward curing cancer's impact on a person's soul. "A merry heart doeth good like a medicine." Proverbs 17:22.

It's like Sarah Addison Allen put so well, "My favorite books are the ones that make me smile for hours after reading them. I want that for my readers, for the sweetness to linger. Sort of like chocolate, but without the calories."

Sophocles said, "There is some pleasure in words, when they bring forgetfulness of present miseries." So, I created a book about why cancer doesn't suck … well, not all the time anyway. Fun times can be experienced when you learn to laugh at yourself.

Open your mind to the possibilities of humor, inspiration, and optimism … and share this book with your "Chemo"Sabes— the newly diagnosed, the survivors, and those praiseworthy caregivers.

AN ANCIENT PRAYER

Give me a good digestion, Lord,
and also something to digest;
Give me a healthy body, Lord, and
sense to keep it at its best.
Give me a healthy mind, good
Lord, to keep the good and pure in
sight;
Which, seeing sin, is not appalled,
but finds a way to set it right.

Give me a mind that is not bound,
that does not whimper, whine, or
sigh.

Don't let me worry over much
about the fussy thing called "I."
Give me a sense of humor, Lord;
give me the grace to see a joke,
To get some happiness from life
and pass it on to other folk.

—Thomas H. B. Webb

GET A TRANSFER

If you are on the Gloomy Line,
Get a transfer.
If you're inclined to fret and pine,
Get a transfer.
Get off the track of doubt and
gloom,
Get on the Sunshine Track—
there's room—
Get a transfer.

If you're on the Worry Train,
Get a transfer.
You must not stay there and
complain,

Get a transfer.
The Cheerful Cars are passing
through,
And there's lots of room for you—
Get a transfer.

If you're on the Grouchy Track,
Get a transfer.
Just take a Happy Special back,
Get a transfer.
Jump on the train and pull the rope,
That lands you at the station of
Hope
Get a transfer.

—Unknown

MISS AMERICA OR MISADVENTURE

"We all have the best laid plans for our children, and they go and ruin it all by growing up any way they want to." —Kristina Riggle

My mother wanted me to be Miss America. I know because she made me watch the annual pageant with her on television. I know because she gave me a Shirley Temple perm when I was five. I know because she made me take tap and ballet at the fine Roy McCollough School of Dance. I hated it. All the prissy details—

crinolines, tapping shoe sounds, makeup, hair bows—and I especially hated tights and tutus!

By age eight, I'd perfected the art of persuasion by listening to my brothers con my parents. Mom gave my hair back to me—no more Shirley Temple perm—and allowed me to quit dance if I agreed to work in my grandmother's grocery store on Saturdays. It was a fair trade; anything to eradicate costumes and lipstick. Plus, I made a dollar a day and ate all the penny candy I wanted.

Mom's expectations for me seemed far-fetched. First of all, the outdoors had me from *Day One*. I loved kickball with the kids on our block. I fished with Daddy when he would put up with someone who wasn't endowed with a pointer to wee-wee off the side of a boat. I rode my bike with cardboard held in place against the spokes with clothespins, eagerly awaiting the day a real motor would putt-putt into my life. When I played outside, I didn't go in until one of my parents honked the car horn three short beeps, signaling nighttime was upon us and I should get my little carcass home.

Other girls learned to play tennis in their cute little skirts. I learned to bowl like the devil, just to impress my famous older brother Jim, the 1963 South Carolina state bowling champ.

While friends took piano and voice lessons, I studied karate. It seemed ultimately more practical. When needed, I could beat the pulp out of somebody—I mean lay 'em flat—instead of hollering like an opera singer, hoping to sing them half to death.

The real deciding factor occurred, however, when Briggs & Stratton built the minibike. This fifteen-year-old curled up into her loving daddy's lap and begged him for motorized wheels. Somehow, he convinced Mom I'd be careful. I was. But, accidents happen. When my foot got caught up under the foot pedal, it bent completely backwards and practically ripped off; it had to be screwed back on. I could never again walk well in heels. My ankle wouldn't quite bend enough. So, there you have it—the crowning blow.

Poor Mom. She wanted Bert Parks to sing for me: "There she is, Miss America." Ah … not so much.

The sad fact is the only thing I had going for me was my hair. I created a flip that could make Mary Tyler Moore jealous. Then, college came with my hippie phase, and my one claim to beauty evaporated like grain alcohol at a fraternity party. I gave up the perfect coiffure for practical wash-and-wear styles.

These styles served me well and saved my babies from hearing some choice words when they upchucked in my hair—words Daddy made famous whenever I'd cast a fishing lure into an oak tree or a brush pile.

I dashed Mom's dreams. She wanted me to be a beautiful, culturally talented lady. I wanted to dissect frogs and solve math equations and break bricks with my hand. You can't perform ballet in bowling shoes. Or show off your new karate gi in the evening gown competition.

I hated to disappoint Mom. We all do. But, can't you just see me now, limping down the aisle in drawstring-waist Karate pants showing off one high heel and one bare foot, accentuating a prominent ankle scar resembling football laces? Can't you picture the shiny yellow bowling shirt sporting my name on the pocket and a 250 Club patch on the sleeve? And Bert Parks singing, "There she goes, Miss Twinkle Toes." Mom, in the audience, would be asking herself, "Where, oh, where did I go wrong?"

Once Mom realized I didn't conform to the mold she planned for me, she allowed me to be me. What a great gift! In the final analysis, she gave me permission to be an individual, which in turn gave me the chutzpah to go boldly into The Big C experience with eyes wide open, asking the doc questions and doing research myself. Never mind the horns, Mom gave me permission to take the bull by the testicles. There's not much one can't accomplish with this mindset.

So, Mom didn't get Miss America for her daughter. Instead, she got a spirited, independent woman who lives to learn, a woman who emotes like nobody's watching, sucking the marrow out of life and daring anyone to find fault with that.

I wonder if Mom was happy with Misadventure, instead of Miss America? When I glide the Hoveround, my last motorized toy, ever so gracefully onto that big *runway in the sky*, totally spent from my misadventures, I'm going to ask her.

THE BRAID OF AFFLICTION

"… after the initial shock and the fear and paranoia and crying and all that goes with cancer … I decided to see what I could do to take that negative and use it in a positive way." —Herbie Mann

After breast cancer diagnosis and surgery, I understood what Granny meant about having her "tit caught in the wringer." Being bald would be tough, too, so I decided to be proactive with a little pep talk: *You're gonna look like your neck is blowing bubble gum in a few weeks, Jan, but you're in charge of how and when you lose your hair.* I was in the driver's seat, if only for a few minutes, with this out-of-control disease.

An epiphany rained down on me in the shower like manna from heaven. This was my chance to sport braids without the usual criticism I endured for my free-spirited nature. Naked and dripping wet, with freshly washed hair in a towel, I dialed a hairstyling salon which specialized in braids.

"Could you cut my hair, then put tiny braids in what's left?"

"Sure, Honey," Linda, the owner of Headhunters Hair Care, said. "When do you wanna come?"

I always admired the long, thin braids worn by African-American women, but I hesitated when the moment for action came.

"Come on now," she said. I liked her enthusiastic voice.

Merrie, the BFF who later

moved into our vacant mother-in-law suite, hauled my stitched-up carcass to the beauty shop. Linda welcomed us at the door with open arms. I explained my situation, created a comfortable nest in the chair, and she assessed the challenge in front of her.

"Ever have this done before?"

"No, ma'am. But I've always wanted to."

"Well, you know you'll need to be here the rest of the day, right?"

"What? You're kidding!"

"No, darlin', I ain't kiddin'. And with your hair … " She picked up a lock between her thumb and forefinger, then grimaced, "this is gonna be a job, ya hear?"

"An all day job?"

She nodded.

"Cheese and crackers! I didn't spend *all day* in the operating room—and I had *four* surgeries."

"Well, if you want this done

right, it'll be an all-day affair." With empathy in her eyes, Linda took my face in her hands. "You up for this, honey?"

Her concern made me wonder if I could muster the stamina. Then *That Still Small Voice* inside spoke to me. Only *my* Jiminy Cricket sounded like Liza Minnelli belting out, "Say 'YES!'"

I laughed out loud. "Yes! Let's do it."

The rubber bands she secured at the roots of my hair caused throbbing pain—the kind your thumb feels when you hit it with a hammer. Then, she braided the locks, threading three red heart beads onto each, and ending with another elastic band.

After four hours, my derriere fell asleep and head hurt so badly I even forgot I'd just had a chunk of my boob cut out. Linda stopped and said, "Go home and rest, sugar. Come back in the mornin' bright and early so we can finish up before you get all tired out again."

I glanced in the mirror. Only half my hair was braided.

"I can't go home like this." Tears welled up. "I'm not done yet."

Merrie laughed, "Don't worry, Jan. We'll put your hat on over it." She eased the knit cap onto my head, which pulled the braids tighter than a strung bow.

"Ow!" I rubbed my head. "These hurt. How am I going to sleep?"

"Best you take some Tylenol before bed," Linda said.

"Tylenol? What good's that gonna do? The hydrocodone I took earlier hasn't dulled *this* pain. Who knew it could hurt so bad?" All the hairdressers snickered at my initiation into their world of beauty. I glanced again in the mirror, then pushed my left eyebrow up to match the right. "Look. These tight braids have pulled my right eyebrow a quarter-inch higher than my left one." My audience found that amusing.

I didn't think so. The pain was overwhelming. I thought for a minute. "You know, I read somewhere about the Jewish bread of affliction being a lesson in humility." I rubbed my head again. "Well, I think this *braid* of affliction will teach me some humility."

After four more hours the next day, my excruciating headache gave way to a deep respect for what my black sisters undergo for their beautiful hairstyles. Sporting four-inch braids bedazzled with red hearts gave me the opportunity to share my story of acceptance, coping, and healing—with just a hint of panache.

The first day of Chemotherapy approached. My hair had grown

just enough to make room for scissors between the scalp and the rubber band. I gathered my daughters, Sarah and Julia, for a special ceremony. Taking matters into their own hands, I believe, helped them deal with my illness.

Sarah snipped off my braids, while my hubby, Irish, videotaped my hair's memorial service. Left with only parted tufts, my head resembled a road map of Downtown, USA.

Julia lined up 106 heart-embellished braids and lovingly reposed each in a small Ziploc coffin along with a card which read:

LOVE IS MY STRENGTH

Unlike Samson, my strength is not in my hair, so I want to share a lock with you as a reminder that my strength comes from the Lord through your diligent prayers. I thank you sincerely.

One heart represents the love I have for you, one represents the love you have for me, and the other represents the Love of God that binds us together.

Not knowing what the future held, but confident Who held the future, I gave these keepsakes to friends and family. Fourteen years have come and gone. Eighteen loved ones who received a braid passed on to their rewards. Seven of those dear souls gave me the honor of holding their hands when the Lord reached out for them.

When diagnosed with Stage II-B breast cancer and four

malignant lymph nodes, I never expected to live this long. The simple faith I gained as a child sustained my journey through the valley, and a positive attitude coupled with a sense of humor smoothed out the rough edges along the way.

Furthermore, my braid of affliction wasn't so bad—after the pain subsided. Not only did I have hair like the amazing Queen Latifah, but also I appeared younger. And why not? My scalp was pulled so tightly my face looked like Dolly Parton after her third facelift ... or fourth ... or whichever.

BASEBALLS, BOOBS, BIOPSIES, AND BELLY LAUGHS

"A well-developed sense of humor is the pole that adds balance to your steps as you walk the tightrope of life." —William Arthur Ward

You want to keep your sanity? Experts say deal with one major event at a time—such as death of a family member, serious illness, mortgage, change in living conditions, revision of personal habits, or a change in recreational or sleeping habits, et cetera.

The new millennium ushered

in so many catastrophes for me that it raised the bar for coping skills. I needed to find humor in my sorry set of circumstances.

Under contract to build a new house with an in-law suite for Mom, my husband Irish and I shared hefty responsibilities. Within weeks of signing the contract, we found out my mother had terminal lung cancer. Mom immediately moved in with us so I could take care of her, but she never saw the completed house. Three months later, ten days before my mother's last Christmas when all her descendants would arrive, I found a lump in my breast.

Lumps are palpable realities. I am an eternal optimist, but my gut told me this was bad. The doc confirmed it, and wanted to do a biopsy right away.

Circumstances compelled me to create the best Christmas of my mom's whole life. No time for surgery. Our extended family shared a reunion etched in our minds forever.

On December 26, I endured the biopsy. On December 28, I weathered the diagnosis: Stage II-B breast cancer. Although I took the news in relative stride, my mother's unsympathetic reaction sliced my heart like a scalpel.

"At least they can cut yours out!"

I guess dealing with her own mortality clouded her judgment and colored her words envy green; or maybe she was just angry at life. But, I expected her to shed tears, as I had when I heard her diagnosis.

When Daddy called Mom's cigarettes *coffin nails* thirty years earlier, I promised not to feel sorry for her when she got lung cancer.

I lied. I wanted more than

anything for chemotherapy to buy her some time, but small cell lung cancer had no known treatment then. She would not lose her hair, but neither would she live to see her next birthday.

Mom died with me by her side ten days before she turned 81. My healthy brothers said they weren't up to speaking at her funeral. Sniveling weaklings! So, sick, puny, and profoundly sad, I delivered her eulogy.

I grieved a long time. I missed my Mommy.

Trying to rescue me from the doldrums, my friend Merrie took me to Whit-Ash Furnishings to choose a recliner for the new house.

Chemotherapy had zapped my strength, and even though we had spent an exhausting, futile afternoon gazing at chairs, I appreciated the sales lady who pampered me. However, when she received a telephone call, she left us in the basement surrounded by about 500 chairs.

I'd learned to take advantage of every opportunity for fun I could find, and this was no exception. I confided in Merrie about a belly-laugh plan. She dared me to do it. That's all it took.

When the clerk came back downstairs she said, "Sorry it took so long, but I probably gave you enough time to choose your favorite chair, right?"

"There are simply too many choices," I said, looking around at 6000 square feet of recliners. "To tell you the truth, I'm so frustrated I'm about to pull out my hair!"

With that, I ripped off my wig.

The poor woman's eyes popped out and her mouth flew open before our laughter filled the ginormous room. Good-hearted laughter often tames the blues, even if it doesn't change the circumstances.

Life throws curve balls. Sometimes a simple curve is welcomed. Sometimes we get a perfect pitch, but don't have our bat ready.

But this time life threw a curve ball with some of the stuffing cut out and extra stitches on the outside. I opened Pandora's box daily. Pandemonium flourished. Limbo ruled. I responded by applying a lesson I learned from my Granny Sheppard: Roll with the tide, don't try to set your watch by it. And, above all, let humor reign.

Janet Sheppard Kelleher

TWO SIZES TOO SMALL

"I do wish my breasts were bigger. Not big ... but less small." — Calista Flockhart

Looking at my chest, one could barely tell I was female even at the ripe old age of fourteen. I'd developed a slightly rounded silhouette by sixteen that improved with a padded bra. The annoying thing was my right boob developed more than my left. There seemed no way to fix it.

Bowling with a twelve-pound ball when I didn't weigh much more myself must have caused my right pectoral muscle to grow, thus creating the illusion of a bigger ta-ta.

Unless I learned to bowl left-handed, I seemed destined to a lopsided life. I never did learn to bowl with my left hand.

Then, I took karate lessons for years along with bowling. Knowing the condition of my bikini stuffers, I tried to learn to punch with my left hand as well as my right. Couldn't. It didn't happen. My durn skinny little right arm threw a serious punch. My right leg was deadly. Confidence exuded everywhere—except my left yabbo.

How would I ever get those pink-nosed puppies equalized?

When I started nursing my first child, he preferred the left milk jug. Aha! We were going to get even now! And, while he sucked down his lunch, I could scarf down mine—with my right hand. Perfect.

An unfortunate thing happened, however. He turned out not to be the only kid who had a strong preference—both of my daughters had the same bias. So, guess what happened after three years of my left jug lactating more milk based on demand from the little rascals? Absolutely! Left coconut bigger than right coconut!

The doctor recommended hormone replacement therapy after my hysterectomy. I wondered if hormones could possibly create a balance. I'd be one lucky kid if so. For the first time since pre-pubescence, could I be *even* keeled?

Not a chance! Not only that, but my yearly mammogram-after-40 showed a mass. Yes, after three short years on HRT, I'd developed a tumor as wide as a ping-pong ball. Bad news, no doubt. BUT—

could it be the answer to the equation? Would it be the equalizer I'd hoped for? Longed for? Can you imagine me cheering for a tumor? If it was in my left breast, making allowances for clean, cancer-free margins should nearly equalize those girls!

No-o-o! The lump grew in my right breast, which meant cutting a serious-sized mass from it. My ta-ta became famous for its resemblance to the Grinch's heart—*two sizes two small!*

Don't get me wrong. I'm a relatively intelligent woman and knew I could've had the size issue improved any time. Having endured all the surgeries I'd suffered in my lifetime, however, I saw no reason for cosmetic surgery. I still had two breasts, be they ever so humble. They worked just fine. I'd been inclined to asymmetry forever, so only the degree changed.

Besides, if God with His sense of humor decided later, in addition to being scared witless that I be boob-less, I might then decide to have fake knockers like Dolly Parton! Until such a time, I chose to remain "unbalanced," which means I require a breast prosthesis to even things out.

Life isn't fair. No one ever said it was. I've dealt with different sized boobs all my life, but at least now I have a prosthesis, which creates the illusion of balance—until I'm stripped naked. Then, what continues to make me laugh is the Pointer Sisters no longer even point in the same direction.

Cheese and Crackers!

Like Norman Rush said, "Small breasts are best for the long haul."

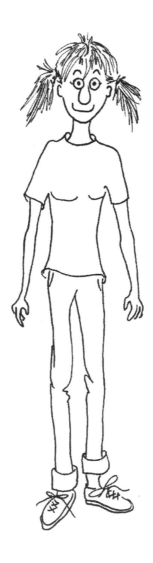

I LEFT MY HEART IN SAN FRANCISCO

"My focus is to forget the pain of life. Forget the pain, mock the pain, reduce it. And laugh." —Jim Carrey

It was all so easy when we were younger. You know, back in the Stone Age. B.C.—Before Chemo. We remembered what to take on a trip, what to buy ahead of time, and could often be packed and ready to go before we walked out the door.

Now, we'd lose our heads if they weren't attached, right? We still have a plan, but it never seems to work out successfully. We make lists, then lose them; wash clothes, then put them away, not remembering they go into the suitcase.

We forget our MapQuest directions and depend on a GPS, which always seems to get lost the last mile of the way.

"Step by step directions are not available."

"WHAT? Don't stop now, right before the climax; I'm almost there!"

Problems abound in the memory department since chemo. I've walked right out the door with my hair resting on its little wig stand, just begging to go to lunch with me.

Misplacing my glasses was a classic, but I now have bifocals and prescription sunglasses, as well as reading glasses and computer glasses, and four times the opportunities to lose them.

I've forgotten my toothbrush; I even had a friend who traveled twenty miles down the road, saw a KFC sign, and realized she'd left her teeth to chatter by themselves in the hotel bathroom drawer. I turned the car around and took her back to the hotel lobby, but I refused to ask the clerk to fetch her teeth!

My daughters bought my friend, Merrie, a padded seat—and by seat, I mean butt. I didn't even know one could buy such things, but it made the perfect Christmas gift and stuffed more than her stocking. Quite pleased with her newfound shapeliness, Merrie took her behind on a cruise in Europe. It fleshed out her rear-end, and her clothes fit better. Until—she got off the boat with it still in the bureau. From that day on; Merrie decided to keep her butt in her own drawers.

I laughed hysterically at my friends' faux pas until I could laugh no more. How could they be so forgetful? Even with chemo brain, I'd never misplaced anything so personal.

My tune changed, however—I got my comeuppance—when I left my fake ta-ta in Atlanta. Now I know I'd even lose my boob if it weren't attached. Comforting, isn't it?

HOME-BREWED TATTOOS

"Life's journey is not to arrive safely at the grave in a well-preserved body, but rather to skid in sideways, totally worn out, shouting, 'Holy Cow, What a Ride!'"
—Hunter S. Thompson

If twenty again, I'd probably be a candidate for tattoos in today's society. And, why not? I wore patches of every description on my jeans in the '70s, making statements like "Feelin' Groovy," "Make Love, Not War," and "Sex Relieves Tension." I paid dearly for my boldness by receiving sermons from my brother George, Granny, Mom, and the best sermonizer yet, Mom's mother, Mamaw.

I am not twenty, however, so I'm telling the story from a sixty-year-old perspective, flavored by a lifetime of living. I've come by my "tattoos" naturally. The story my unwrapped body tells is more colorful and soulful than my '70s streaking bod could ever imagine.

The idea of home-brewed tattoos hit shortly after surgery. With the drain out of my side, the doctor allowed a shower. I removed my glasses, had help pulling off my clothes, and turned on that delicious WaterPik. I preferred Calgon to "take me away," but a soaking bath continued to be only a wish.

The long-awaited first shower after surgery defined refreshing. I felt it wash away pre-surgery anxiety and betadine prep, along with post-surgery blood, goo, and guts. A new start—phase one treatment was behind me. Recovery, then chemotherapy, more recovery, radiation, and then more recovery.

Weakness from chemo led to extra careful measures while doing any activity, so bosom buddy Merrie—second layer of skin— helped with the first of many showers. She responded to every need, sometimes before I even knew I had a need.

I exited the shower stall and pawed for a towel. Merrie ordered me to turn around. She draped the towel around my shoulders and patted me dry like a little kid. I caught a glimpse of myself in the full-length mirror. Then, I stared. I spied scars literally from head to foot—on both feet, in fact.

My body was a roadmap.

Each track told the story of a place I'd visited and of the journey traveled.

Acne scars wove a story of teenage angst, insecurity, and unruly hormones.

Right breast and pit scars offered testimony to my cancer journey and kinship to an aunt on Dad's side. They also screamed, "Hormone replacement therapy feeds some cancers!"

Left breast scars told of fibrocystic disease. Hereditary in nature, benign cysts invaded an aunt on Mom's side and me. Nothing earth shattering, but we should avoid caffeine. *Uh-huh. Sure thing, Doc.*

The ribcage scar spoke of another familial problem. Lipoma, a benign tumor, left a scar like big brother George sported, and I was proud of it!

The belly scar told the tale of

a baby who did NOT want to leave the comfort of the womb, the associated decision to shut down the baby factory, and drugs that rendered me speechless to report pain during the C-section.

The left knee scar evidenced a mid-life crisis relationship with my Honda Nighthawk motorcycle, for which Mom comforted me with, "I told you so!"

The right knee scars explained a doctor's attempt at repairing damaged cartilage from years of karate demonstrations and bowling antics.

The left ankle scar represented a mini-bike at age sixteen, the rescue by my riding buddy, Paula, lying x-rays which showed nothing broken, my first bone fracture, and understanding teachers.

The humor of it all finally slapped me in the face. Thank

God. At times, humor is priceless. I dropped the towel to the floor and laughed out loud, while Merrie scratched her head and tried to assess the situation.

"Don't you see?" I said. "I should make thank-you notes with a picture of exactly what I see in the mirror. Caption: 'Count Your Blessings. Things could be a lot worse … you could look like THIS!'"

Home-brewed tattoos, not the ink-and-needle version, tell the real story of a person. Like author Garrison Keillor said, "It's a shallow life that doesn't give a person a few scars." With the number I've been supplied, I believe my guardian angel is saying, "You see, Jan, you've really had A Wonderful Life!"

THE TATTERED TA-TA

"Anyone can be passionate, but it takes real lovers to be silly."—Rose Franken

Although battered and tattered, it mattered.

So, I asked Irish, my Yankee husband, "What do you do with a tattered ta-ta?"

His answer proved that a metamorphosis had taken place in South Carolina. Sunshine, moonshine, and Spanish moss finally and completely transfused his blood. And it only took forty years!

In the chaos of packing for a roadtrip to see Aretha Franklin, I required a last-minute bag. Among the things jammed together before we left was my perky silicone prosthesis. Why I didn't wear the mammary masquerade that day is beyond me.

After arriving in Tennessee, I watched in horror as Irish unloaded the van, dropping the calfskin bag onto the sidewalk. My heart fell. I grabbed the tote and charged into the condo to examine the abused cargo. My worst fear was realized. The hairdryer plug had stabbed my spare hooter. *Psycho's* staccato theme pulsed through my brain as I imagined silicone oozing down the drain at the Bates Motel.

Then I experienced an epiphany—genuine appreciation of Granny's tales of tits caught in wringers gushed forth like silicone from my mangled boob. A "booboo!" But, what could I do to fix it?

I went back to the parking lot, with problem literally in hand, to ask my engineer husband, "What have you done? I can't see the Queen of Soul like this!"

He continued to unpack. "Like what?"

Gnashing teeth with the intensity of Sally Field portraying *Sybil,* I resisted the urge to flip him off behind his back. "Stop. And pay attention!"

He turned and ogled the pseudo-boob, my bosom balancer, then asked, "What the heck happened to that?"

"What's it look like, Irish? You punctured my prosthesis!"

"Wait a dang minute ... *you* packed it."

"But *you* slammed it into the pavement."

Arguing only made matters worse. I glanced down at my

bustline. A tight turtleneck accentuated the difference between my naturally Lilliputian girls—one orange-sized, the other tangerine-sized. I sniveled.

"What am I gonna do?"

A genuine rocket scientist by profession, Irish could figure out a quick solution to my dilemma, I just knew it. He gestured with his hands as if playing with a Slinky. "Can't you just stuff a sock in your bra? That should balance out the ol' boobs."

No doubt about it, I was doomed. "That's not funny, genius. You need a little R-E-S-P-E-C-T."

Properly shamed, Irish ruminated a moment. Then, with a blatant disregard for his scientific skills, his Yankee ingenuity mated with his acquired redneck resourcefulness right there in the parking lot in front of God and everybody.

"I've got it!" he said, with the mischievous grin of a leprechaun. "Give me that pink-nosed puppy."

Using his favorite "tool" from the van emergency kit, Irish went to work. Within minutes my sweet, *desperate* husband (in an attempt to redeem himself) expertly engineered the duct-taped-ta-ta. Don't reckon you can get any more Southern than that!

THINGS TO REMEMBER

"Some days there won't be a song in your heart. Sing anyway." — Emory Austin

"Finally, brethren, whatsoever things are true, whatsoever things are honest, whatsoever things are just, whatsoever things are pure, whatsoever things are lovely, whatsoever things are of good report; if there be any virtue, and if there be any praise, think on these things." —KJV, Philippians 4:8

Read humorous books.

It's like Mamaw always said, "Want in one hand and spit in the other, and see which one fills up the quickest!" Therefore, when you desire something, it's not enough to want it so badly you can taste it. You have to get off your duff and out of your comfort zone to get it.

The key to survival is early detection. Keep abreast of cancer. Have a regular mammogram.

Read *A Call to Character.*

A grilled hot dog bar and banana split bar make a perfect summer party menu for people of all ages.

Read the New Testament from cover to cover.

People in your vocation or avocation who are willing to give you a leg up are worth their weight in gold.

If you could manufacture the equivalent of what the neighbor's Don Juan Doggie leaves in our yard that causes our Chihuahua to go out in the Arctic air to get a whiff, you could develop a perfume that would make people forget the name Chanel.

No matter how illogical it might be, sometimes crying uncontrollably is the only response to a situation. You need to go through your emotions to get to the other side.

Don't waste time and energy trying to understand how or why you got cancer. Concentrate on getting better. Realize what an incredible creation your body is. Focus on the positive.

Put on your big girl panties and deal with it.

Picture yourself healthy again.

Watch funny movies.

You can put Alka-Seltzer in a martini glass or a soda fountain glass, doesn't matter. It still tastes like marsh water.

Your dog loves you unconditionally

—even if you scold him, give him a weekly bath, and take away his favorite chicken jerky treats because they were recalled.

You can throw your back out with one good "Aaaaaa-choooo!"

Keep your weight down. Fat cells produce estrogen. Estrogen makes tumors grow.

Caught without sugar and cream? A half pack of instant cocoa in your coffee works wonders.

A random act of kindness sometimes renders the recipient speechless. Do it often just to enjoy their reaction.

Multi-tasking is for the young. Old people fumble. We put our shoes in the refrigerator and our butter under the bed. And sometimes, we swallow an earplug, thinking it's a glucosamine and chondroitin supplement.

Surround yourself with positive people.

After tasting sashimi/sushi, I know why man discovered fire! God never intended baitfish to be eaten raw by anybody.

Reading how-to books can take you just so far; then you actually have to do the activity to learn how. And, the more frequently you do it, the better you become.

I've lived so long and had so many surgeries that, if I've still got it, it hurts!

My laptop can beat me at solitaire, but I can beat the devil out of it at karate!

Janet Sheppard Kelleher

IT COULDN'T BE DONE

Somebody said that it couldn't be done

But he with a chuckle replied

That "maybe it couldn't," but he would be one

Who wouldn't say so till he'd tried.

So he buckled right in with the trace of a grin

On his face. If he worried he hid it.

He started to sing as he tackled the thing

That couldn't be done, and he did it!

Somebody scoffed: "Oh, you'll never do that;

At least no one ever has done it;"

But he took off his coat and he took off his hat

And the first thing we knew he'd begun it.

With a lift of his chin and a bit of a grin,

Without any doubting or quiddit,

He started to sing as he tackled the thing

That couldn't be done, and he did it.

There are thousands to tell you it cannot be done,

There are thousands to prophesy
failure,

There are thousands to point out to
you one by one,

The dangers that wait to assail you.

But just buckle in with a bit of a
grin,

Just take off your coat and go to it;

Just start in to sing as you tackle
the thing

That "cannot be done," and you'll
do it.

—Edgar Albert Guest

Janet Sheppard Kelleher

I'LL CONTINUE TO BUY GREEN BANANAS

My current plan is to get flattened one day by a Budweiser truck while crossing the street with my old fart cane … the sports model I have with the rear view mirror, air horn, and change purse, which carries bribe money for the cop who stops me for shuffling along too fast for my condition!

But, until then …

I turned a new decade last year—kissed my fifties goodbye.

I'm pretty excited about this latter part of my life. If I'm allowed the Biblical "three score and ten," I'll be a *long*-term breast cancer survivor. Either way, I'm sliding into the home stretch, making the most of every day. Just think: no matter what I accomplish from now on, I'll be able to encourage others by saying, "Of course, you should try this. I'm over sixty, and I did it!"

I'll make new friends, because at my age I lose them often—and friends are good to have. They're the family God doesn't give you, but you find along the way.

I'll make a list of this past year's accomplishments and milestones, and create a list of the bombs also just to get that off my chest.

Then, *write down* my goals, because accomplishments first need a plan and then a plan of attack. Setting goals means I intend to do something.

If you haven't done this, preparing a bucket list is always a nice place to start—a list of things you want to do, as well as a list of ways you want to *be*. For example, I *want* to be less emotional. That is a tall order, but not impossible. The thing is, I have heretofore been unsuccessful in convincing myself that it's illogical to cry, so my immediate reaction to news—good or bad—is always visceral. Tears of joy bleed as freely as tears of sadness.

I won't sit around and wait for things to happen, I'll take charge and make them happen. In so doing, I must remember to allow room for mistakes. Mistakes mean I'm trying, not quitting. Dealing with consequences is part of the learning process. Learning is wising up, and wising up means growing!

I will try new things, and do the best with what I have. Recognize my limitations, but not put up limits unnecessarily. S-t-r-e-t-c-h.

I will no longer worry that my best might not be good enough. If it's my best, by golly, it *IS* good enough. We all have strengths and weaknesses. I'll be tolerant of others' weaknesses, too.

Whatever life has been thus far, I cannot change a thing about it now. I'm going to grab the remainder by the testicles—after all, I have my own mother's permission—live, love, laugh, and learn like each day is all I have. Forgive like it's my last chance. It just might be. Seek out and take advantage of opportunity. Make a difference where I am; and, when it's all evaluated at the last Trump, I'll look back without regrets.

Quoting Erma Bombeck, the

famous columnist and breast cancer survivor, "When I stand before God at the end of my life, I would hope that I would not have a single bit of talent left, and could say, 'I used everything you gave me.'"

For posterity's sake, I included blank pages at the end of this memoir. Jot down the "funny" you find on your journey. It will help open your mind to the possibilities of humor and point to the positive. God bless and keep you, my fellow "Chemo"Sabes!

Now go Kick Breast Cancer's Butt!

ABOUT THE AUTHOR

Janet Sheppard Kelleher, a breast cancer victor since 2000, is an award-winning creative nonfiction writer, columnist, and speaker. Enjoy her stories in multiple issues of *Not Your Mother's Books*, *Chicken Soup for the Soul*, *The Petigru Review*, and more. Her "Havin' My Cotton-Pickin' Say" newspaper column has appeared in The *Hampton County Guardian* and The *Jasper County Sun.*

Jan has won numerous writing awards including the Carrie McCray Memorial Award for Nonfiction; the Southeastern Writers Association Award for Excellence in Inspirational Writing; the Microcosm Award; The Past Loves Day Contest; the Hal Bernard Memorial Award for

Nonfiction; and the Morton J. Rubin Limerick Award, Southeastern Writers Association.

Jan lives with her husband Irish in West Columbia, South Carolina. An empty-nester mother of three children, she enjoys traveling, exploring old ruins, archaeology, hunting, fishing, parasailing, ballooning, reading, Sudoku and crossword puzzles, golden oldies, and volunteering for causes close to her heart. Jan received a Bachelor of Arts in Mathematics from Sweet Briar College, VA.

Keep up with Jan at www.JanetSheppardKelleher.com or find Janet Sheppard Kelleher on Facebook for the latest news, contests, personal appearances, and new book releases.

Connect with her via About.Me/JanetSheppardKelleher.

Big C, little ta-ta

Janet Sheppard Kelleher

Big C, little ta-ta

Janet Sheppard Kelleher

34198824R00053

Made in the USA
San Bernardino, CA
01 May 2019